MY ANCES٦

QUAKERS

HOW CAN I FIND OUT MORE ABOUT THEM?

Edward H Milligan

Malcom J Thomas

Society of Genealogists

Published by the
Society of Genealogists
14 Charterhouse Buildings
Goswell Road
London EC1M 7BA
Registered Charity No. 233701

First published 1983
Reprinted 1990

This edition published 1999

ISBN 1 85951 404 9

FOREWORD

This book is designedly modest in scope. It attempts to do little more than outline the structure of meetings for church affairs of the Religious Society of Friends in Britain and Ireland, and indicate the main classes of records produced by those meetings and likely to be of interest to the genealogist and family historian. Many books, portions of books, and articles would carry the researcher further but considerations of space prevent full documentation of these. Particular reference should, however, be made to Donald J. Steel, *Sources for nonconformist genealogy and family history* (National index of parish registers vol. 2), 1973, pp. 601-695. Family history, local history and social history are closely inter-related and it is hoped that this guide will be serviceable to the local historian.

The Society of Friends is a religious community. It exists in order to worship God and to witness to those insights (whether on issues of peace, race relations, social justice, or whatever else) which it has found through its experience of corporate search. The Society has throughout its history sought to be meticulous in the keeping of records (whatever shortcomings there may have been in practice) and recognises that it stands as trustee in relation to those records. The Society is not, as such, interested in genealogy, though many of its members over the years have found it an absorbing subject. There are many applications of the words of Isaiah: 'Look unto the rock whence ye are hewn and to the hole of the pit whence ye are digged'.

Though we have mentioned some sources relating to the twentieth century we have not reckoned to attempt more than to guide the searcher to sources available up to about 1900. In attempting brevity we have recognised that in any effort at simplification there is always the danger of over-simplification, so that many of our statements require caveats that do not appear. There are also rival dates for various events where it would have needed a reasoned statement to explain our choice. In a publication of this kind there are bound, even in this revised and enlarged edition, to be errors which have escaped our notice. We are grateful to all those (whom we forbear to name) who have commented on our initial drafts or the 1983 publication: the present revision is better for their help, but responsibility for what now appears is ours alone. We would welcome further comments and proposed alterations, in case there should be a yet further edition - or even just for our own benefit.

EDWARD H. MILLIGAN

MALCOLM J. THOMAS

Friends House Library

Euston Road, London NW1 2BJ

TABLE OF CONTENTS

STRUCTURE OF MEETINGS FOR CHURCH AFFAIRS

WOMEN'S MEETINGS

APPENDICES

A Digest registers: explanation of contents; lists of the 1840-2 quarterly meetings

B Dates in pre-1752 Quaker documents

C London yearly meeting queries 1742

D Transcripts of minute books

E Editions of the book of discipline to 1900

F Adoptions

INSTITUTIONS AND SOCIETIES

1   **Britain and Ireland** The Library of the Society of Friends (Friends House, Euston Road, London NW1 2BJ; tel: 0171-663 1135; e-mail: library@quaker.org.uk; Web: htpp://www.quaker.org.uk) is the first point of contact. In addition to its own holdings it can offer guidance on other sources, for instance the whereabouts of local minute books deposited in county or other record offices. For Ireland the counterpart is Friends Historical Library (Swanbrook House, Bloomfield Avenue, Dublin 4; tel: 00 3531 6687157). An obvious contact is the Society of Genealogists (14 Charterhouse Buildings, Goswell Road, London EC1M 7BA; tel: 0171-251 8799). Friends Historical Society (c/o Library of the Society of Friends) has since 1903 published a *Journal*, a typescript index to which is in two sequences (1903-53, 1954-75) and available at Friends House Library. The Quaker Family History Society (c/o 32 Ashburnham Road, Ampthill, Beds MK45 2RH; e-mail: qfhs@cwcom.net; Web: htpp://www.qfhs.mcmail.com) has since 1994 published *Quaker connections*, which includes regular notes and queries on work in progress.

2   **Overseas** In North America the libraries of first instance are The Quaker Collection, Haverford College Library (Haverford, PA 19041, USA: tel: 001-215 896 1161) and Friends Historical Library, Swarthmore College, 9500 College Avenue, Swarthmore, PA 19081-1399, USA: tel: 001-215 328 8496). Friends Historical Association (c/o Haverford College Library) publishes *Bulletin of the Friends Historical Society of Philadelphia* (1906-1923*), Bulletin of the Friends Historical Association* (1924-1961), *Quaker history* (1962 onwards). While mainly American in emphasis the journal is not entirely so: it contains many articles of transatlantic significance. Quinquennial printed indexes are published. The North Carolina Friends Historical Society (PO Box 8502, Greensboro, NC 27419-0502, USA) has since 1979 published *The southern Friend*, and the Canadian Friends Historical Association (Friends House, 60 Lowther Avenue, Toronto, Ontario, Canada M5R 1C7) since 1972 *The Canadian Quaker history journal (*until 1990 *newsletter)*. Enquiries about institutions and historical societies elsewhere should be made at Friends House Library.

QUAKER ORIGINS AND ORGANISATION

3   Origins Quakerism arose in the English east midlands in the late 1640s, gathering momentum in the north in the early 1650s. From 1654 it spread to the south of England and to the continent of Europe (§71), the West Indies and North America (§§69-70). If puritanism is understood as a belief that the Elizabethan settlement had not gone far enough, then Quakerism may be seen as puritanism taken almost to its logical conclusion. At the same time it was a reaction against (and was seen as dangerous by) those puritans who had stopped at a mid-way position. The frequent assumption that Quakers had anything to do with the pilgrim fathers or, in particular, the voyage of the *Mayflower* (1620) is plainly wrong. As early as 1654 a local meeting for church affairs had been set up in county Durham. Local, regional and national conferences were held in the ensuing years and in England and Wales were established in a regular system from 1667-9. In and after 1670 meetings for church affairs were started in America.

4   Structure in England For the most part Quaker meetings for church affairs (earlier known as meetings for discipline) in England ran, from the 1660s until the end of 1966, on a four tier system:-

a   The preparative meeting (§19) being a meeting for church affairs in relation to a single meeting for worship or sometimes a group of such meetings (it may be compared to a parish).

b   The monthly meeting (§20), normally comprising a number of local meetings: the monthly meeting was and is the principal meeting for church affairs in the Society, its responsibilities including membership and (normally) property (it may be compared, if the likeness be not pressed too far, to a rural deanery).

c   The quarterly meeting (§22), initially covering a single county and normally comprising between two and seven monthly meetings, was often in the position of a court of appeal in relation to them, exercising also a pastoral responsibility over them (it may be compared to a diocese).

d   The yearly meeting (§28) comprised Friends from the English quarterly meetings with representatives from the yearly meetings for Wales (§25) and in Scotland (§26), from the national half yearly meeting for Ireland (§27) and accredited visitors from overseas (it may be compared to a province - or to the provinces of Canterbury and York united).

Conscious of meeting under the guidance of the holy spirit they had (and have) neither president nor chairman but a clerk, whose task it was (and is) to present the business and, as the sense of the meeting emerged, to encapsulate it in a minute drawn up, altered as necessary, and approved at the time.

5   **Variations** What is outlined above is subject to a number of variations in different places. In particular, there are a number of exceptions in relation to Wales, Scotland and Ireland (§§25-7). Meetings for church affairs at every level produced numerous records. For anyone looking for a Quaker name, however, the starting point is nearly always the registers. It may be useful, therefore, to describe the registers before amplifying on the Society's administrative structure.

BIRTH, MARRIAGE AND BURIAL REGISTERS: ENGLAND and WALES

6   **Background** Register books began to be kept by Quaker meetings from the late 1650s. The registers record births (not baptisms, since Friends do not observe the outward sacraments), marriages and burials (normally, but not always, with date of death). When some birth registers were begun, the adult members of the meeting meticulously recorded their own dates of birth, so that one register has a retrospective entry as early as 1575. In general, responsibility for registers rested with the area monthly meeting, but in practice local registers were sometimes also maintained. From 1776 there was a more systematic registration, printed books being provided for monthly and quarterly meetings. Register books ceased on 30 June 1837. Great care should be exercised in relation to all dates up to the end of 1751; see appendix B.

7   Surrender of registers Following the Registration Act 1836 and Marriage Act 1836 came the Non-Parochial Registers Act 1840 (3 & 4 Vict. c. 92) under this some 1,445 registers (together with notes and certificates) were surrendered to the Registrar General so that they might be used in courts of justice as evidence. Friends made duplicate digests of the registers before their surrender (§11). A further surrender of 121 registers took place in 1857, digests again being made. All these original registers are now at the Public Record Office, Kew, as part of class RG6, and a new and more accurate description and listing of them was made by the PRO in 1997.

8   Unsurrendered registers Some registers, intended to be transferred under the Non-Parochial Registers Act, were in the event returned to Friends, because they did not qualify under the act. Besides these, various registers have come to light since the second surrender in 1857, having been in family hands or in other ways out of official custody. An early Thetford (Norfolk) register and the Whitby and Scarborough register are now in the care of Friends House Library, and others may have found their way into county or other record offices, or still remain in private hands.

9   Missing registers Since the administration of the Society's meetings for church affairs was in the hands of private individuals it is not surprising that, in the course of time, completed minute books and registers became mislaid, particularly where the meeting was closed on account of emigration or other causes. It would be possible and perhaps desirable, though labourious, to reconstruct years for which a register book for any given monthly meeting ought to have existed

10 Deficiencies in entry The fact that an entry in a register book ought to exist does not mean that it does. For example, Buckinghamshire quarterly meeting noted in 1709 that for several years past three of its four constituent monthly meetings had not brought in proper accounts of marriages, births and burials. In the fourth monthly meeting (Upperside), Rebecca Butterfield records in her diary her attendance at 66 interments at Jordans between 1746 and 1776: only 12 of these are in the registers. The reputation of Friends for full and efficient registration is not as justified as could be wished.

11 Digest registers The digests made by the Society in 1840-2, at the time of surrender, were not transcripts. The registers relating to meetings within each of the then quarterly meetings in England and Wales had their contents systematically arranged so that, under each letter of the alphabet, entries in each series – that is births, marriages, burials - appear in approximately chronological order from the 17th century to 1837. (A very few entries in some areas go up to 1841, but such later entries are mainly in the supplements taken from originals surrendered in 1857.) Witnesses to marriages whose names appear in the original registers (§58) were not transcribed in the digest. The digests were made in duplicate, one copy being retained centrally (now in Friends House Library) and the other returned to the quarterly meeting. Further information on the arrangement of material in the digests, and on the whereabouts of the quarterly meeting copy, will be found in appendix A.

12 Deficiencies in digest registers An account of the preparation of the digest registers is given in *J. Friends Hist. Soc. vol. 30, 1933, pp. 50-5*. In view of the working conditions of the copyists and the fact that they were not trained palaeographers, it is impressive that the digests are as accurate as they are. Nevertheless, recent research by Harold Greenwood has shown that, while it is almost true to say that a record of each vital event was transferred to the digest, (a) the copyists did not include references back to every record of the event; and (b) they did omit a few, admittedly almost illegible, entries.

13 Copies of digest registers A microfilm of the digest registers for England and Wales (32 reels) is on public sale: enquiry should be made of Friends House Library. Copies of the microfilm are available for consultation there and at the Society of Genealogists. Many county and other record offices have the reel(s) relating to their area. Typescript copies of register entries, though often relating to specific quarterly meetings and/or limited to specified years, are available for consultation at Friends House Library and the Society of Genealogists: they relate to some 500 families, as indexed. The Quaker Family History Society, in consultation with Friends House Library committee, has embarked on a database of all entries in the digest registers for England and Wales. A printout in three alphabetical sequences (births, marriages, burials) is available at Friends House

Library and the Society of Genealogists for Essex QM, Suffolk QM and (shortly) Norfolk and Norwich QM. Offers of help in the project should be directed in the first instance to Friends House Library.

14 Post-1837 registers One of the effects of the Registration Act 1836 had been to increase record-consciousness. One result in the Society of Friends was the decision to supply each monthly meeting with a book to serve as a manuscript register of members, to be kept from 1 July 1837 (§53). Another was the supply of a more regular form of birth note and burial note, effective from the same date. Yearly meeting 1860 asked monthly meetings to supply information from their birth and burial notes, and from their marriage registers, so that post-1837 digests might be compiled. Provision was made for annual returns in future so that the digests might be kept up. London yearly meeting abolished birthright membership as from 31 December 1959 and the digest of births ends at that point. For a variety of reasons, Meeting for Sufferings decided to discontinue the digest of deaths as from 31 December 1961.

15 Omissions from post-1837 digests Some of the omissions from the post-1837 digests are due simply to human error. Three forms of omission, however, arise from the Society's regulations and should be mentioned:-

a.Birthright membership was available, for most of the period under review, only to children both of whose parents were in membership at the time of birth.

b.Where both parents are known to have been in membership at the time of marriage and it appears that some children have not been recorded, this may be because one or both parents were at the relevant time disowned persons (perhaps later reinstated).

c.Responsibility for producing a burial note lay not with the monthly meeting of which the deceased was a member but with the monthly meeting in the compass of which interment took place, and as the use of public cemeteries (and, later, crematoria) increased so the chance that the responsible monthly meeting was aware of its responsibilities diminished.

BIRTH, MARRIAGE AND BURIAL REGISTERS: SCOTLAND, IRELAND

16 Scotland In Scotland meetings for church affairs were not always regularly held and until 1786 registration was sporadic. The Registration, Marriage and Non-Parochial Registers Acts did not apply to Scotland, and so the question of the surrender of registers did not arise. In 1867, however, an arrangement was made between Meeting for Sufferings and the general meeting for Scotland for the compilation of a digest on the lines of the pre-1837 digests for England and Wales, and annual returns from monthly meetings in Scotland from 1867 are included in the post-1837 digests. A list of all names in both register books and minute books within Edinburgh yearly meeting to 1790, compiled by William F. Miller, is available in Friends House Library: it contains some names of Friends within Aberdeen yearly meeting.

17 Ireland Since the Non-Parochial Registers Act did not apply to Ireland, the registers (as in Scotland) continued to be kept with the quarterly or monthly meeting records. A particular feature of the Irish records was the compilation of 'family lists', enabling a very ready check of the generations of a given family within the same monthly meeting, usually with reference to marriages of children. Volumes of abstracts of all births, marriages and burials up to 1859 were compiled by Ireland yearly meeting and are at Friends Historical Library, Dublin, which also houses the Webb pedigrees and Jones index. Thomas Henry Webb (1844-1925) compiled from the registers typed pedigree sheets for 232 families while, later, Isabel Jones listed every surname occurring in the registers, showing the monthly meeting(s) in which the name occurred. A list of over 2,250 surnames (including variant spellings) which occur in Irish Quaker registers will be found in Olive C. Goodbody, *Guide to Irish Quaker records 1654-1860*, 1967, pp. 193-207.

STRUCTURE OF MEETINGS FOR CHURCH AFFAIRS

18 Extent and location It will now be useful to expand on the structure of Quaker meetings for church affairs. In general, men and women met separately for business until 1896 (but see §37). The majority of local Quaker records up to the late 19th century are deposited in local record offices or in university libraries; some remain in local meeting houses; those for the area of London and Middlesex quarterly meeting are in Friends House Library, which maintains a catalogue of the whereabouts of other local records. Although the quantity of records may at first sight seem considerable, the size of relevant records at local level is not likely to be daunting. It is the monthly meeting records which are likely to be most helpful after the digest registers have been examined. The brief notes that follow may usefully be supplemented in 'Meetings for church affairs within Britain yearly meeting' by Jean Mortimer, in *Quaker connections* no. 11, July 1997, pp. 9-17, no. 12, Nov. 1997, pp. 7-13, where actual examples illustrate the types of business transacted.

19 Preparative meetings (§4a) In the south of England and the midlands few preparative meetings existed before the 1760s: their business was to 'prepare for the monthly meeting', mainly by drawing up, for the monthly meeting preceding the quarterly meeting, answers to the queries (§29). They often met only four times a year with no further record than the minute book recording the answers. On occasion the women's preparative meeting acted in a pastoral and relief capacity and minutes sometimes record gifts of money or coals, or similar information. In the north of England, and in isolated places in the south, where a meeting was at some distance from the main centre of the monthly meeting, preparative meetings tended to be established earlier, some minutes being extant from the 1690s: such meetings often assumed more responsibility for finance and property and minutes are correspondingly fuller, account books and other records sometimes being kept as well. Such preparative meetings are, especially before the mid-18th century, sometimes confusingly referred to as monthly meetings.

20 Monthly meetings (§4b) In 1694 there were 151 monthly meetings in England and Wales; in 1800, 108; in 1900, 68; in 1998, also 68. Because of the pressure of business, City of London or Bull and Mouth (later Gracechurch Street) was initially a two weeks meeting, as was Colchester until 1759 and Bristol until 1784. The monthly meeting's responsibilities included finance and property matters (§§66-8); general questions of discipline (which might arise from answers to the queries); oversight of marriages (§§55-6); recording sufferings (§63); arrangements for apprenticeship; poor relief; and matters relating to membership (§§46-54). The minutes of the men's meeting (the principal series) may be expected to record all such business; for the women's minutes see §37, and for ministers and elders' minutes see §45.

21 Monthly meeting minutes: transcripts For three quarterly meetings (Berkshire, Somerset, Wiltshire) the 17th century, and in some cases early 18th century, minutes have been transcribed *in extenso* and indexed. Where transcripts exist, it proves far easier to follow an episode through both quarterly and monthly meetings and more such transcripts are much to be desired. For a list of existing transcripts, see appendix D.

22 Quarterly meetings (§4c) In the 17th century there was a quarterly meeting for virtually every county in England. Following a general visitation of the country in the years following 1760, a process began by which quarterly meetings were amalgamated. In 1797 the yearly meeting for Wales (§25) became a half-year's meeting with the functions of a quarterly meeting, so that in 1800 there were effectively 29 quarterly meetings in England and Wales; in 1900, 17; and in 1966, 18. From 1 January 1967 the functions of quarterly meetings were considerably curtailed and they were renamed general meetings: they no longer were part of the system described in §4, which thus became in effect a three-tier system.

Up to 1700, and in some places later, there was no hard and fast line between monthly and quarterly meeting business, cases of difficulty often coming to whichever meeting happened soonest. Gradually quarterly meetings developed a function as a court of appeal, taking action when monthly meetings reported exceptions in their answers to the queries (§29) and hearing appeals by Friends against monthly meeting proceedings, notably in the case of disownment (§50). The minutes of the men's meeting (the principal series) may be expected to record all such business; for the women's minutes see §37, and for ministers' and elders' minutes see §45. A working index to London and Middlesex quarterly meeting minutes 1671-1868, compiled from contemporary indexes to each minute book, is available in Friends House Library. For transcripts of quarterly meeting minutes, see appendix D.

23 Six weeks meeting In 1671 a meeting was settled in London confined to 'grave and antient Friends' to consider 'things not fit to be discoursed about' in more open meetings for church affairs. It was a court of appeal from monthly meetings, 'the prime meeting of the city' though its later responsibilities were mainly with London finance and property. Disownments (§50) were reported to it until 1825: this is particularly relevant in the case of Gracechurch Street monthly meeting, whose records were destroyed by fire in 1821. A working index to its minutes 1671-1868, compiled from the contemporary indexes to each minute book, is available in Friends House Library; a typed transcript of minutes 1671-1692/3 is also available. For further information, see William Beck and T. Frederick Ball, *The London Friends' meetings*, 1869, pp. 91- 133; Winifred M. White, *Six weeks meeting 1671-1971*, 1971.

24 Yearly meetings The phrase 'yearly meeting' was used in relation to a regular meeting for church affairs, an annual gathering which was also a meeting of record, and an annual gathering which was not a meeting of record (see §§25-8, 32-4 for examples). Besides these, other occasions, usually widely-publicised meetings for worship with the attendance of ministering Friends, were known as 'yearly meetings', and are referred to in this way in 18th century documents: examples are Colchester yearly meeting; Norwich yearly meeting; or the successive meetings at Hertford, Hitchin and Baldock which 'are held in course and are called yearly meetings at this season of the year (June)' (Robert Willis, quoted in Henry J. Cadbury, *John Woolman in England* (Friends Historical Society supplement 32), 1971, p. 76). Care should be taken not to confuse these various 'yearly meetings' with the appointed meetings for church affairs. Before considering London yearly meeting (the annual gathering of Friends in Britain) it will be relevant to outline the general situation in Wales, Scotland and Ireland.

25 Structure in Wales A yearly meeting for Wales was established in 1668 with three quarterly meetings: (a) North Wales, which comprised Merionethshire, Montgomeryshire and Shropshire; (b) South Wales, which comprised Pembrokeshire, Carmarthenshire and Glamorgan; and (c) Monmouthshire, which later included Radnorshire. The few Friends in Denbighshire were attached to Cheshire QM. The relationship between the yearly meeting for Wales and London yearly meeting was ambivalent: Wales sent London a 'foreign epistle' as a co-equal but answered the queries and sent representatives as a subordinate. In 1797 the quarterly meetings were abolished and the yearly meeting transformed into Wales half years meeting, having the status of a quarterly meeting: in 1832 the half years meeting was joined to Hereford and Worcester quarterly meeting under the style of Hereford, Worcester and Wales general meeting (so styled because it met fewer than four times a year). Emigration from Wales to Pennsylvania in the 17th and 18th centuries was considerable, whole meetings being depleted. This may be one reason for the considerable deficiencies in the records of births, marriages and burials and in certain other records (§9).

26 Structure in Scotland Because of the problems of distance and the small number of Friends in Scotland, the system of meetings for church affairs described in §4 did not obtain. Meetings for discipline were usually held for each of the meetings which had sufficient strength to need and to sustain organisation. These local meetings were loosely associated with the yearly meeting at Aberdeen or the yearly meeting at Edinburgh: leading Friends in Scotland regarded themselves as members of either or both yearly meetings, each of which sent an epistle to London. By the 1780s the discipline had broken down altogether and in 1786 the half years meeting for North Britain was established, having virtually the functions of a quarterly meeting: in 1807 the half years meeting was renamed the general meeting for Scotland. From 1786 there were two monthly meetings, each of which at one stage or another in its life was styled a two months meeting. A helpful interim guide to sources is provided in 'Towards a bibliography for students of

Scottish Quaker family history' by John H. Gray, in *Quaker connections* no. 11, July 1997, pp. 119-24, no. 12, March 1998, pp. 10-6.

27 Structure in Ireland Friends in Ireland were, until 1797, organised in a three-tier structure: (a) the monthly meeting; (b) the province meeting; and (c) the national meeting. Having said that however, there are more caveats to be made than in England. The national meeting was a half yearly meeting, always held in Dublin, and it tended to consider matters of detail far more than did London yearly meeting. By the 19th century the half yearly meeting had ceased to send London yearly meeting its answers to the queries. The province meetings were in many cases barely distinguishable from monthly meetings. The province meeting for Munster, for instance, was held as a six weeks meeting, while County Tipperary monthly meeting was also held as a six weeks meeting so that a meeting for church affairs was held every three weeks. Nor was it quite as simple as that, for at one period County Tipperary monthly meeting and Waterford monthly meeting attempted to hold a joint six weeks meeting alternating with province meetings, while Cork monthly meeting was held as a three weeks meeting. In Leinster province there were fewer complications, though the pre-eminence of Dublin men's meeting should be noted. In Ulster province the precise relationship between local worshipping groups and monthly meetings was not always clear. There was no province meeting for Connaught. In 1797 the half yearly meeting became the yearly meeting of Friends in Ireland (commonly called Dublin yearly meeting until 1949), the province meetings were renamed quarterly meetings, and a body known as the yearly meeting's committee was established to deal with business in the interim between yearly meetings.

28 London yearly meeting (§4d) The yearly meeting of the Society of Friends in Great Britain had the style 'London yearly meeting' because until its first meeting in the provinces in 1905 it had met unbrokenly in that city. Its style was changed, as from 1995, to 'Britain yearly meeting'. Its purpose was defined in its epistle of 1718 as 'for a great and weighty oversight and Christian care of the affairs of the churches pertaining to our holy profession and Christian communion'. One way in which it exercised this was through the consideration of the quarterly meeting answers to the queries. Its normal order of agenda was:-

names of representatives (§31); accounts of sufferings (§64); answers to queries (§29); epistles received from other yearly meetings (§72); consideration of 'Truth's prosperity' (later, 'the state of the Society'); and propositions from quarterly meetings. It also received, but normally did not minute in detail, appeals of individual Friends or of monthly meetings against quarterly meeting decisions. A working index for 1672-1856, compiled from contemporary indexes to each minute book, is available in Friends House Library.

29 London yearly meeting queries In 1682 London yearly meeting asked quarterly and monthly meetings three questions (Yearly meeting minutes vol. 1 p. 115):

1 What Friends in the Ministry, in their respective Counties, departed this Life since the last Yearly Meeting?

2 What friends Imprisoned for their Testimony have dyed in Prison since the last Yearly Meeting'?

3 How the Truth has prospered amongst them since the last Yearly Meeting, and how friends are in Peace and Unity?

These questions (to which others were added) were answered annually and recorded in the yearly meeting minutes (from 1791 retained in the yearly meeting papers). Gradually the tone changed: the questions became queries, designed to ensure that the membership was upholding Quaker testimonies - against tithes, or being concerned in war and for 'plainness of speech, behaviour and apparel' (for 1742 queries, see appendix C). Those Friends not upholding these testimonies might come 'under dealing' to the point, if necessary, of disownment - a responsibility of the monthly meeting (§50). Besides the yearly meeting queries, several quarterly meetings (§22) drew up their own queries: these were codified in 1755 and abolished in 1790. There were also separate queries for women's meetings and for meetings of ministers and elders.

30 The book of discipline Deficiencies reported in the answers to the queries, or enquiries from local Friends as to whether certain practices were or were not 'in accordance with Truth', led London yearly meeting to issue advices as appropriate. By the 1730s the need of some codification was felt and, in 1738, yearly meeting issued a manuscript volume 'Christian and brotherly advices'. Revisions have been made at intervals of roughly a generation ever since, and reference to the work has tended to be to the 'book of extracts' or, later, 'book of discipline'. Since there is not only advice but detailed regulations on procedure, the relevant volume is essential for an intelligent understanding of minute books. As Friends in Ireland moved into increasing independence, that yearly meeting in the 19th century began to issue its own book of discipline. Editions of successive revisions by London and Ireland yearly meetings are listed in appendix E.

31 Yearly meeting representatives Until 1861 London yearly meeting was technically comprised only of the quarterly meeting representatives, such ministering Friends as might be in town (§40), and the members or correspondents of the Meeting for Sufferings (§36), with certain other provisions relating to Wales, Scotland and Ireland (§§25-7). In fact, however, other Friends attended in increasing numbers and in 1861 the meeting was constitutionally opened to all men Friends, women later being included and the separate women's yearly meeting being laid down in 1907. Lists of 6,000 men representatives of 1668-1861, arranged chronologically and alphabetically, are available in Friends House Library.

32 Bristol yearly meeting (1695-1798) Established by London yearly meeting, this yearly meeting was in part a meeting for discipline and of record, receiving answers to its queries from the quarterly meetings in the west of England. It also provided an opportunity, through meetings for worship largely attended by non-Friends, for Friends travelling in the ministry (§41) not only to sustain the membership but also to spread the Quaker concept of the Christian message.

33 Northern yearly meeting (1699-1798) In part a meeting for discipline and of record, the northern yearly meeting was established to comprise the quarterly meetings of Cheshire, Lancashire, Westmorland and Cumberland, and it circulated in its place of meeting. Perhaps its more important function was, like Bristol and the western circular yearly meetings, to provide an opportunity for making the Quaker message widely known. For further information, including a list of places where it met, see 'The circulating yearly meeting for the northern counties 1699-1798' by David M. Butler, in *J. Friends Hist. Soc.* vol. 52 (1968-71) pp. 192-202.

34 Western circular yearly meeting (1720-1786) Established at the instance of Bristol yearly meeting, the circular yearly meeting was never a meeting for discipline, its function being, like Bristol and the northern yearly meetings, to provide an opportunity for making the Quaker message widely known. For further information, including a list of dates and places where it met, see 'Western circular yearly meeting 1720-1786' by Russell S. Mortimer, in *J. Friends Hist. Soc.* vol. 39 (1947) pp. 33-4.

35 Fritchley general meeting (1869-1968) After a number of 'meetings for conference' in the early 1860s, Fritchley general meeting with a constituent monthly meeting, was established by a number of Friends in Derbyshire and elsewhere who were dissatisfied with the innovations of doctrine and practice within London yearly meeting. Births, marriages and burials in the records of Fritchley monthly meeting are listed in Walter Lowndes, *The Quakers of Fritchley 1863-1980*, 1980, revised ed., 1986.

36 Meeting for Sufferings Following a conference in the autumn of 1675 a 'constant meeting about sufferings' was established, the series of minutes beginning in June 1676. It dealt with 'cases of suffering' anywhere in Britain, and for this purpose it had a network of county correspondents who were in a position to bring to light cases where the prosecution might have been illegal. It met weekly until the late 18th century and was entrusted with more and more work of a general nature, being defined by London yearly meeting 1833 as 'a standing committee of this meeting ... entrusted with a general care of whatever may arise during the intervals of this meeting, affecting our religious society and requiring immediate attention', a definition which still stands. A working index for 1700-1857, compiled from contemporary indexes to each minute book, is available in Friends House Library.

WOMEN'S MEETINGS

37 General A number of women's monthly and quarterly meetings had been established from the 1670s. Their minutes, while more variable than those of the men's meeting in what they record, are often worth consulting for poor relief and membership matters relating to women Friends, and also for enquiries as to clearness from other engagements of women Friends intending marriage. In the 19th century women and men increasingly met together in preparative meetings, and in the latter half of the century for at least part of monthly and quarterly meetings. By 1896, 24 monthly meetings in Britain and two in Ireland were held wholly jointly. From that year all in Britain were so held, though, additionally, women's monthly meetings continued to be held in some areas until at least the 1920s.

38 Box meeting The women's two weeks and box meetings (the latter being primarily for poor relief) had their origin as early as 1659. They were meetings of London women Friends but undertook certain national responsibilities, such as corresponding with women Friends overseas. The meeting of the women's two weeks and box meetings held at the time of London yearly meeting was attended by women Friends from throughout the nation and provided opportunity for national conference, minutes being kept from 1759. For further information, see 'The women Friends of London: the two-weeks and box meetings' by Irene L. Edwards, in *J. Friends Hist. Soc.* vol. 47 (1955) pp. 3-21.

39 London women's yearly meeting (1785-1907) It was not until 1784 that a women's yearly meeting was formally constituted, with power to communicate with women's quarterly meetings: it first met in this capacity in 1785. In the latter part of the 19th century joint sessions of London yearly meeting were increasingly held and in 1896 women Friends were constitutionally recognised as equal members of that yearly meeting. A separate women's yearly meeting continued until 1907. For further information, including a list of clerks of the meeting, see 'The women's yearly meeting' by Mary Jane Godlee, in London yearly meeting during 250 years, 1919, pp. 93-122, 135-7, 143-4.

MINISTERS, ELDERS, OVERSEERS
AND THEIR MEETINGS

40 Ministers Out of the expectant silence of Quaker worship, vocal ministry might (and may) be given by any one of the worshippers, under the leadings of the holy spirit. It was early recognised that the gift of vocal ministry was given in greater measure to some than to others, and these (men and women) came to be known as 'publick Friends' (that is Friends who might preach the gospel and give a public testimony to their faith). In the early 18th century a more systematic form of recognition by monthly meetings was seen to be desirable and the Friends so recognised were known as 'acknowledged' or 'recorded' ministers. The practice of recording was abolished by decision of London yearly meeting 1924.

41 Liberation for religious service To guard against Friends 'rambling up and down the country' unacceptably, the practice grew up whereby it was expected that a Friend travelling 'in the ministry' either in this country or abroad should seek the unity of his or her monthly meeting, which would then draw up a 'certificate of liberation' for the Friend to carry as evidence of credentials. Where the service was outside Britain the certificate was endorsed by the quarterly meeting and by London yearly meeting (§28) or, from the mid-18th century, the yearly meeting of ministers and elders (§45) or, between yearly meetings, the second day morning meeting (§44). American ministers visiting Britain carried similar credentials and it was the duty of the yearly meeting of ministers and elders or the second day morning meeting to issue a 'returning certificate' on the completion of their service.

42 Ministers deceased The 1682 question 1 (§29) or 1742 query 5 (appendix C) asked for annual returns to yearly meetings of ministers deceased. A chronological list for 1700-1843 is available in Friends House Library together with a typescript alphabetical index. For some of these ministers a longer 'testimony' was prepared, designed to show the workings of divine grace in human life. Earlier testimonies were copied in the 'Book of ministering Friends', a manuscript not now extant. A new series 'Testimonies concerning ministers deceased' (7 vol., 1728-1872) contains, also, from the early 19th century, minutes respecting some elders deceased. Yearly meeting 1861 empowered monthly meetings to prepare a testimony concerning any deceased Friend, where this seemed appropriate. An index to 2,460 testimonies presented to yearly meeting 1728-1982 is available in Friends House Library.

43 Elders; overseers The word 'elder' appears in Quaker documents from Commonwealth days (for example 'To the elders and faithful brethren of the north'): here it means a seasoned Friend - had not Quakers a dislike for the phrase, we might say 'one of the leadership'. The specific appointment by monthly meetings of elders 'to counsel ministers' belongs to the first half of the 18th century. From the late 17th century overseers had been appointed to have a care for Friends in want and to watch over the remiss, since the injunction of Paul, 'Withdraw yourselves from every brother that walketh disorderly' (II Thess. 3: 6) was taken with due seriousness (see §50 for dealing and disownment). Though by 1755 a quarterly meeting query (§§22, 29) asked. 'Have you two or more faithful Friends deputed in each particular meeting, to have the oversight thereof?' there was, at least in some cases, confusion on the distinction between elders and overseers until as late as 1789 when London yearly meeting made a firm ruling.

44 Morning meeting (1673-1901) From the 1660s, if not earlier, it had been the custom of 'publick Friends' (§40) to meet together in the City of London, deciding and recording which meeting for worship each should attend. Subsequently, a meeting on second-day (Monday) morning enabled them to compare notes and to confer together on matters of common concern. The meeting was formally established by 1673, its functions including the consideration of manuscripts intended to be printed. It was also responsible for liberating Friends for religious service (§41) in the intervals between yearly meetings. During the 19th century its activities steadily declined and its remaining functions were transferred to Meeting for Sufferings (§36) in 1901. An index to its minutes 1673-1901, together with those of the yearly meeting of ministers and elders 1754-1906 (§45), is available in Friends House Library.

45 Meetings of ministers and elders From the mid-18th century monthly and quarterly meetings of ministers and elders began to be generally held: their minutes not infrequently record the presence of visiting ministering Friends where no record is to be found in the corresponding minutes of the men's monthly meeting. The yearly meeting of ministers and elders was instituted in 1754, though for some years the sitting of the second day morning meeting (§44) held at the time of yearly meeting virtually acted in this capacity. Later, preparative meetings of ministers and elders were held in a few places, mainly in larger meetings. These bodies are often referred to as 'select' (for example 'the select quarterly meeting'). In 1876 overseers and other Friends appointed by the monthly meeting were admitted, and the select meetings were known as meetings on ministry and oversight. They were laid down by decision of yearly meeting 1906 but continued in a few places as committees on ministry and oversight.

MEMBERSHIP

46 General It is sometimes claimed that during the first half century of Quakerism there was no formal membership in the Society. This is not so. A concept of formal membership existed from very near the beginnings of Quakerism: the entry of children's names in the birth register, consent for marriage according to Quaker usage, the receipt of poor relief, interment in a Quaker burial ground - all these were clear, if ad hoc, recognition of membership. Indeed, poor relief was sometimes given to a person 'not as a Friend but as an object of pity'. In 1737 London yearly meeting adopted lengthy 'rules for removals and settlement' which set out, following principles akin to the poor law, what facts enabled a Friend to gain a settlement in a monthly meeting, which thus became responsible for his or her relief. In general, it was about the mid-18th century that procedures were adopted for formal admission of those 'under convincement' (§48). A few words of elaboration on membership matters may be useful.

47 Births Children, both of whose parents were in membership at the time of birth, had until 1959 a right to membership. Other children might be admitted as minors at the request of the parents. Since Friends maintained a testimony against water baptism, no record is to be expected in parish registers, though occasionally incumbents felt it a civic duty to record all births in the parish. During certain periods, particularly 1776-1837, non-member children who had some claim to be under the care of Friends are entered in the registers, distinguished by NM. In general this tended to be where one parent only was in membership: in some cases, however, 'NM' was entered where neither parent appears to have been in membership - perhaps because one parent had been disowned for marriage before the priest to a non-Friend.

48 Convincements In most places it was not until the mid-18th century that procedures were adopted for formal admission of those under convincement. Record of appointment to a particular duty, of application to be married according to Quaker usage, or of removal, may therefore be the first indication that a Friend has been 'received by convincement'.

49 Removals Although, from the 1670s, it had been customary for Friends moving from one monthly meeting to any other to carry with them a certificate (later, the certificate was sent direct from one monthly meeting to the other), it was not until the mid-18th century that it became general to record outgoing certificates, and in many cases incoming certificates were kept on file but not minuted. It is important to recognise that for many emigrants there will therefore be no specific mention of removal in British Quaker records and, very often, none in American local records either. During the 19th century a number of monthly meetings at different times adopted the practice of dealing with removals by entry in a certificate book, again without record in the monthly meeting minutes. It should also be remembered that a certificate might not be sent until, perhaps, years after the time of removal, particularly if the Friend was 'under dealing' (§50) or in receipt of poor relief.

50 Disownments Among disownable offences were:- habitually absenting oneself from meetings for worship; drinking to excess; commercial dishonesty, including most cases of bankruptcy; having a bastard child or a child conceived before wedlock; paying tithes; being concerned in war (for example having armed vessels, joining the army or hiring a substitute for the militia); marriage before a priest, or being present at such a marriage. The matter was normally reported to monthly meeting which would appoint Friends to examine the circumstances, referring to the women's meeting if necessary. If, after receiving the report, the monthly meeting decided to disown, the minute of disownment normally recited the full circumstances and was copied in the minutes or in a separate book. In the London monthly meetings the disownment was until 1825 reported to the six weeks meeting (§23).

51 Reinstatements It is important to bear in mind that disownment did not involve exclusion from meetings for worship, and those who continued to attend might, after a decent interval, be reinstated. For most of the period under review, discipline provided that this should be done by the disowning monthly meeting. It will sometimes therefore be found that the disowning monthly meeting made enquiries of the monthly meeting in which the disowned person lived before proceeding to reinstatement. After reinstatement, the disowning monthly meeting may well send a certificate of removal, whose date may bear no relation to the date of the actual move.

52 Deaths Friends could not, and in any case would not, have their bodies interred in consecrated ground and therefore provided their own burial grounds (§68). Entries in parish registers are occasionally to be found, however, either because the incumbent felt it a civic duty to record all births in the parish or a legal duty to record that the burial had been in woollen. Friends testified against mourning and other 'vain funeral customs'. Where a death is not to be found in the registers, it can sometimes be deduced from a bequest recorded in monthly meeting minutes or similar circumstantial evidence. In the 20th century cremation was increasingly adopted and in the latter half of the century there were few interments.

53 Registers of members There are few regularly-kept registers of members before 1812: but they were in general use from 1837. The terminal dates of these 1837 registers vary widely. Indexes to the initial 1837 registers of 14 monthly meetings are available in Friends House Library. In some registers at some periods the entry under 'death' records not the date of death but the date of report to monthly meeting: caution should therefore be used. The official registers of members are to be distinguished from the privately-printed lists issued by monthly and quarterly meetings from the latter part of the 19th century.

54 Attenders and associates In addition to those in membership there are non-members described as attenders or (in a few places between 1899 and 1966) associates. Friends in the later 19th and early 20th centuries were considerably involved in adult schools and mission meetings either on their premises or otherwise closely associated: comparatively few of those attending adult schools or mission meetings joined the Society and therefore do not appear in official Quaker records.

MARRIAGE

55 Procedure During the Commonwealth Friends adopted declarations before witnesses akin to those in the marriage ceremony of the 1644 *Directory of publique worship*, but (as might be expected) denied the need for priest or minister. The continuance of this procedure after the Restoration meant that, in the eyes of the church, there was no marriage and any issue was illegitimate: a consequence was that non-Friend relatives could and did contest wills (Quaker wills were proved before the relevant ecclesiastical court in the usual way: see §86). The civil law, however, in judgements given from 1661 onwards held that marriages according to Quaker usage were good marriages. Friends were at pains to develop (a) a system of adequate preliminaries; (b) an open ceremony with a certificate signed by the parties and a maximum number of witnesses; and (c) an efficient system of registration. This procedure is described in detail in Edward H. Milligan, *Quaker marriage*, 1994, but the main outline is given below.

56 Declarations of intention The couple declared their intentions of marriage at two successive sessions of the monthly meeting(s) to which they belonged. When satisfied that both parties were free of other engagements, the monthly meeting to which the woman belonged liberated them to make their declarations of commitment in a public meeting for worship. Special arrangements applied in London (§57). The minutes recording the declarations may often contain information on parentage and occupation not recorded in the registers. From declarations of intention it may also be possible to deduce marriages which are not found in the registers, but do not assume that a marriage took place merely because the minutes contain such declarations.

57 Two weeks meeting In addition to its capacity as a meeting for church affairs, the City (London) or Bull and Mouth two weeks meeting appears to have assumed, or caused a second body to assume, general oversight for the six London monthly meetings in relation to marriage: this continued until 1789 as the responsibility of a body with no other specific function. The minutes for 1672-1789 are particularly useful in tracking the marriage of a London Friend to a Friend living elsewhere: a typescript index to them is available in Friends House Library. For further information on the two weeks meeting, see William Beck and T. Frederick Ball, *The London Friends' meetings*, 1869, pp. 85-91.

58 Registration It should be noted that, for earlier marriages, the original registers often list the names of witnesses, whereas the digest registers (§ 11) do not. The certificate was (and is) retained by the parties, though some meetings kept file copies. From the early 18th century the certificate usually gave the names of parents and is thus, if traceable, potentially important if their names are not given either in the declarations of intention or in the registers. Since 'the world's people' might well be present at a marriage, the name of a witness on a certificate is no proof of membership. For a substantial period a separate column of the certificate was headed 'relatives'.

59 Legislation: England and Wales While Quaker marriages had thus been recognised in common law, Friends were at pains to draw the attention of parliament to the good order of Quaker proceedings, with a view to recognition in statute law. A statement of procedure, including the text of the marriage certificate, was circulated to members of parliament at the time of the 1690 bill on clandestine marriages, and again in 1718 when a further bill was before parliament. Continuing efforts were made, resulting in implicit recognition in Lord Hardwicke's Act of 1753 (26 Geo. 2 c. 33) which contained a clause excepting Quakers and Jews 'where both the Parties to any such Marriage shall be of the People called Quakers, or Persons professing the Jewish Religion respectively'. The Marriage Act 1836 (6 & 7 Will. 4 c. 85) explicitly recognised Quaker marriages but with the same proviso as Lord Hardwicke's Act. It was not until the Marriage (Society of Friends) Act 1860 (25 & 26 Vict. c. 18), passed at the instance of yearly meeting 1859, that marriages according to Quaker usage could be contracted by those 'professing with Friends'. This provision was later extended to any non-member approved by the Society's proper officers through the Marriage (Society of Friends) Act 1872 (35 & 36 Vict. c. 10).

60 Legislation: Ireland, Scotland The Marriage (Ireland) Act 1844 (7 & 8 Vict. c. 81) established registration districts on lines similar to those for England and Wales: it also made similar provision for Quaker marriages. These provisions were extended by the Marriage (Society of Friends) Acts 1860 and 1872. The Registration of Births Deaths and Marriages (Scotland) Act 1854 (17 & 18 Vict. c. 80) established similar registration districts for Scotland and provided that a marriage schedule from a district registrar be presented, in the case of Quaker marriages, to 'the responsible person'. The Marriage (Society of Friends) Acts 1860 and 1872, did not apply to Scotland. The 1844 and 1854 acts made clear in statute law the legality of Quaker marriages in those two countries.

61 'Disownment for marrying out' Quakers, having rejected 'the hireling priesthood', could not countenance the marriage of a Friend before the priest. This was equally true whether the marriage were to another Friend or to a non-Friend. Where both were Friends they not infrequently 'ran off to the priest' either because of an insuperable difficulty in the discipline (lack of parents' consent; marriage of first cousins), or because the protracted nature of the Quaker preliminaries was irksome (and if there was a child conceived out of wedlock disownment might take place anyway). As far as marriage to a non-Friend was concerned, marriage according to Quaker usage was not legally possible in England and Wales or in Ireland until 1860 or 1872 (see §59) and in Scotland not until 1939. From 1837 marriage before the Superintendent Registrar had been possible but this, while not open to the same objections, ran counter to Quaker conviction that 'marriage is a religious ordinance and not a mere civil compact'. After 1860 those married before a priest were still liable to disownment: it should be noted that different monthly meetings ceased to disown at different dates until about the end of the 19th century. It will be seen that technically there was no such thing as 'disownment for marrying out'; but 'marrying out' legally involved, for a long period, marriage before the priest, which was a disownable offence.

SUFFERINGS

62 Legislation   There was sporadic (but sometimes severe) persecution of Quakers during the Commonwealth. But after the Restoration in 1660 a series of enactments penalised all dissenters. Quakers were prosecuted particularly for not going to church; holding meetings of five or more 'under the pretence or colour of worship'; refusal to swear an oath; refusal to pay tithes, church rates and other customary dues; opening their shops on first-days (Sundays) and holidays; travelling on first-day; being vagabonds or common nuisances; contempt of courts and magistrates (for example, by refusal to remove their hats) and teaching without a bishop's licence. They could be prosecuted under common law, canon law, or statute law: among the statutes Quakers particularly complained about were the Quaker Act 1662, the Conventicle Acts 1664 and 1670 (the latter giving the common informer sweeping powers), and the recusancy acts of Elizabeth I and James I (originally passed against Roman Catholics), under which Friends were liable to fines of £20 per month and possible loss of land. The Toleration Act 1689, passed early in the reign of William and Mary, granted freedom of worship to dissenters under prescribed conditions. Friends were still distrained upon for non-payment of tithes, and incurred penalties under the 18th century militia acts.

63 Monthly and quarterly meeting records   All cases of prosecution or distraint were in theory recorded in a series of books of sufferings, kept by monthly and quarterly meetings and by yearly meeting: these contain useful information on such non-Friends as informers, priests, constables and justices. In some cases the monthly or quarterly meeting book is not extant. In others, sufferings may not have been copied into the monthly meeting book by the time it was urgent to take them to the quarterly meeting. No one book should be assumed to be the definitive one. From 1793 standard printed books were supplied to quarterly and monthly meetings for their use.

64 'Great book of sufferings' Returns of sufferings as brought to London yearly meeting by quarterly meeting representatives can be found in the 'Great book of sufferings' (1650-1856 in 44 volumes). The 29 volumes up to 1791 are copied in manuscript and indexed (the index does not after the earliest volumes contain the names of informers, priests, justices, etc.). From 1791, to ensure entries in standard form, there are printed sheets for these returns to the yearly meeting, which are inevitably more formal. An index to all names of Friends, as recorded in volumes 1 - 29 (1650-1791) is in active preparation and will be available in Friends House Library.

65 Printed sources From the outset, Friends were assiduous in printing tracts and broadsides about their persecution. A list of 250 such publications up to 1700 will be found in Joseph Smith, *A descriptive catalogue of Friends' books*, 1867, vol. 2, pp. 644-83. In the 1730s, Meeting for Sufferings (§36) entrusted Joseph Besse with the task of summarising entries from volumes 1 and 2 of the great book of sufferings (that is, up to 1689). He had published in octavo *An abstract of the sufferings of the people call'd Quakers* (3 vol., 1733-8) when Meeting for Sufferings decided on a different arrangement and he started afresh. The result was the folio *A collection of the sufferings of the people called Quakers* (2 vol., 1753), arranged by county (and country overseas). Volume 2 contains 15 indexes. A reduced size facsimile edition of the Yorkshire section has been published as *Sufferings of early Quakers in Yorkshire, 1652 to 1690*, 1998, with much fuller indexes of persons and places by Michael Gandy. It is hoped that this will meet a need and justify similar facsimile reprints for other counties. Such a facsimile for Berkshire, with person and place indexes by Elizabeth Longhurst, is available at Friends House Library.

FINANCE AND PROPERTY

66 Account books Monthly meeting minutes until the early or mid-18th century usually provide summary (and sometimes detailed) accounts of money collected and disbursed. From these, or separate account books, and records of collections, whether for the monthly meeting stock or a special purpose (for example the building of a meeting house) it is usually possible to judge the relative affluence of a Friend; while the disbursements may indicate a needy Friend, whether temporarily in emergency or long-term. Financial grants to needy women Friends were often in the hands of the women's monthly meeting. The records of the Meeting of twelve are a (largely untapped) source of information on the finances of London Quakerism. Turning to the yearly meeting, its national stock accounts, where extant, may contain quite detailed analysis of the expenditure of Friends travelling in the ministry overseas.

67 Meeting houses It is sometimes believed that Friends had to wait till the Toleration Act 1689 before they could build meeting houses. This is far from the case. Besides adaptations, there had been many purpose-built meeting houses during the previous two decades, though farmhouses and other private dwellings continued to be used, as registrations under the Toleration Act show. Deeds and trust property books will prove useful in determining those in a meeting considered of sufficient substance to be appointed trustees. For a general survey, see David M. Butler, *Quaker meeting houses*, 1995. A full description of all known meeting houses, extant or otherwise, with bibliographical references, will be found in David M. Butler, *The meeting houses of Britain*, 2 vol., 1999.

68 Burial grounds From the outset Quakers possessed their own burial grounds, which very often antedate meeting houses or are entirely separate from them. Their siting was usually a matter of chance, not choice: most were initially the gift of a local Friend and, if he were a farmer, it would be reasonable for him to give that portion of his land least useful for agricultural purposes. Nor was a burial ground necessarily used, some Friends making use of their own orchard or garden. While gravestones were sometimes erected in the 17th and early 18th centuries, they were far from universal. London yearly meeting noted in 1717 that the 'vain custom' obtained in some places, and asked that such stones be removed and that no others should be set up. The advice was reiterated in 1766, and very few of these earlier gravestones can now be seen. In 1850 London yearly meeting agreed that graves might be marked by 'a plain stone, the inscription on which is confined to a simple record of the name, age, and date of the decease, of the individual interred'. In the years following, a number of such stones were erected in relation to those who had died previous to 1850. Friends have seldom felt a sentimental attachment to burial grounds. In country districts especially many have been sold, particularly where they have been remote from any meeting. While plans were kept of burial grounds in use, these were not always preserved after burial grounds went out of use, Friends having little if any veneration for 'last resting places'. In very many burial grounds the post 1850 headstones have now been moved to (for instance) the burial ground walls.

FRIENDS OVERSEAS

69 17th century North America Between 1655 and 1662 about 60 Quaker missionaries arrived in the New World, where they made converts and established meetings. Their main centres of activity were New England (particularly Rhode Island), New Amsterdam (later New York) and Long Island, Maryland, Virginia, and the West Indies. A number of Friends developed financial interests in East and West New Jersey, and in 1682 William Penn's constitution for Pennsylvania was adopted. By the end of the 17th century autonomous yearly meetings were in existence for New England, Maryland, Philadelphia, New York, Virginia and North Carolina. A sense of Atlantic community was fostered by the regular exchange of epistles (§72) between London and yearly meetings (and other less formally organised groups) overseas, and by Friends 'travelling in the ministry' (§73).

70 Emigration to North America Emigration to North America in the latter part of the 17th and in the early 18th centuries was on a considerable scale. Particular reference should be made to William Wade Hinshaw, *Encyclopaedia of Quaker genealogy*, 7 vol., 1936-1970 (now available on CD-ROM). It should be noted, however, that the titles of the volumes (1 North Carolina, 2 Philadelphia, 3 New York, 4 and 5 Ohio, 6 Virginia, 7 Indiana) are not a full description of their contents, since not all monthly meeting minutes within the relevant yearly meetings have been examined and the years covered vary. It is, however, an invaluable work. Some supplements have been produced. As far as Philadelphia is concerned, incoming certificates of removal are listed in Albert Cook Myers,

Quaker arrivals at Philadelphia 1682-1750, 1902. The Irish entries in this are reprinted, with considerable further material, in his *Immigration of the Irish Quakers into Pennsylvania, 1682-1750, with their early history in Ireland*, 1902 (reprint published by Heritage Books, Bowie, Maryland. 1998). Some of the emigrants from Wales are listed in T. Mardy Rees, *Quakers in Wales*, 1925. Until the mid-18th century, the issue of a certificate is unlikely to be minuted by a monthly meeting in Britain (§ 49). The *Pennsylvania magazine of history and biography*, published in Philadelphia from 1877, contains many references to Friends who emigrated from the British Isles to America. A printed index to vol. 1-75 (1877-1951) has been published.

71 Continent of Europe The first Friends to journey on the continent sailed in 1654. There was little or no response in the greater part of Europe, but in the Netherlands, Friedrichstadt and Dantzig flourishing communities grew, though comparatively few records have survived. The results of the 17th century initiative on the continent had virtually died out by the mid-18th century, the last epistle to London from the yearly meeting in Amsterdam being in 1788. During the 1780s, however, Quakers in Britain came into contact with a mystical group of some 150 members in and around Congénies, in the south of France, and similar groups in Germany, centred on Pyrmont and Minden, and two months meetings for church affairs were established. These groups, and others established as Norway (1846) and Denmark (1875) yearly meetings, had died out or were reduced to a handful by the end of the 19th century.

72 Epistles London yearly meeting maintained volumes of 'Epistles received' (9 vol., 1683-1897) and 'Epistles sent' (9 vol., 1683-1916): these are available on microfilm. Until towards the end of the 18th century, epistles from America (§69) and elsewhere were generally signed by a substantial number of Friends present. Increasingly from the 18th century they were signed only by the clerk (§4). An inventory of vol. 1-5 (1683-1799) of the series 'Epistles received', together with an index of signatories, is available in Friends House Library.

73 Ministerial travels Up to the end of the 19th century, at least 450 Friends, British, Irish and American (quite apart from merchants on business), crossed the

Atlantic 'under religious concern'. Their visits were extensive and sometimes involved their being away from home for a year or more. A number of these Friends crossed the Atlantic several times. An index entitled 'Quaker transatlantic journeys' is available in Friends House Library, listing British and American ministers liberated for overseas service: it is arranged chronologically with an index of names.

74 Australasia; South Africa Quaker settlers reached Australia from the early 19th century. Between 1832 and 1861 meetings were established at Hobart, Adelaide, Melbourne and Sydney: in 1861 London yearly meeting recognised the first three as monthly meetings, further meetings and monthly meetings being later established. Up to 1861, some 1,000 Quaker emigrants from Britain and Ireland had settled in Australia (many in fact being disowned Friends): 'A biographical index of Quakers in Australia before 1862' (1982, revisions, 1984, 1986), compiled by William and Marjorie Oats, is available in Friends House Library and in Friends Historical Library, Dublin. William N. Oats, *A question of survival: Quakers in Australia in the nineteenth century*, 1985, lists (pp. 50-9) these names, many being treated in the course of his text, and also the names of visiting Friends who, in many cases, listed those Australian Friends they met. Australia yearly meeting now produces annual supplements to a Dictionary of Australian Quaker biography, which is, like the Dictionary of Quaker biography (§87), very much a working document. Files are available at a number of libraries in Australia, at Friends House Library, at the Brotherton Library of the University of Leeds, and at Haverford and Swarthmore Colleges, Pennsylvania.

Though there had been Quaker settlers in New Zealand from the 1840s, it was the mid-1880s before a meeting (Auckland) was established on a regular basis. Similarly, in South Africa, Quaker settlers were widely scattered and Cape Town meeting was not firmly established until 1904. Hope Hay Hewison, *Hedge of wild almonds: South Africa, the pro-Boers and the Quaker conscience, 1890-1910*, 1989, covers, in fact, earlier events and refers to most Quakers who settled in or visited the country in the 19th century. New Zealand Friends have since 1988 published a series entitled 'Quaker historical manuscripts'.

75 Continental committee Meeting for Sufferings in 1817 appointed a committee to correspond with Friends in Pyrmont and Minden (§ 71). It soon expanded its field to include Congénies and, later, other groups on the continent of Europe, in Australasia, Calcutta, southern Africa, and other places. Its papers include numerous references to individuals, and the volume 'Casual correspondence' records official letters to and from these groups. Responsibility for some of its work was transferred in 1903 to the Australia (from 1908, Australasia) committee and the South African Relief Fund (from 1908, South African) committee. The Continental committee was laid down in 1920.

76 Missionary work Quakers long held aloof from missionary work, fearing a compromise with their testimony against 'a hireling ministry'. In 1868 an independent Friends Foreign Mission Association was formed, taking responsibility for work in India (1866), Madagascar (1867), China (1886) and Ceylon (1896). In 1899 it took over the work of the Friends Syrian Mission (1874) and in 1918 that of the Pemba Industrial Mission (1896). In 1927 the FFMA was amalgamated into the Friends Service Council. Typescript indexes are available in Friends House Library of missionaries with the FFMA 1868-1927 (300 names) and of workers with the Friends Service Council 1927-1978 (1,000 names).

77 Relief and ambulance work Between 1914 and 1924 some 2,000 people served with the Friends War Victims Relief (from 1919, Emergency and War Victims Relief) committee, which worked in France, Holland, Russia, Poland, Austria and Germany: a list will be found in A. Ruth Fry, *A Quaker adventure*, 1926, pp. 357-378. There were some 1,700 members of a Friends Ambulance Unit 1914-9, largely engaged on hospital trains in France but with a home section: their names are given in Meaburn Tatham and James E. Miles, *The Friends' Ambulance Unit 1914-1919*, [1920], pp. 252-263. In the second world war 1,300 men and women served with a revived FAU (1939-46) in Britain, Finland, north Africa, Ethiopia, Syria, China, India, Greece, Italy and north-west Europe: a list will be found in A. Tegla Davies, *Friends Ambulance Unit...1939-46*, 1947, pp. 467-481. A Friends War Victims Relief (from 1943, Friends Relief Service) committee (1940-8) had 1,200 people working with it in Britain, France, Palestine, East Africa, Gibraltar, Casablanca, Italy, Greece, Germany, Holland, Austria and

Poland: a list is given in Roger C. Wilson, *Quaker relief. . .1940-1948*, 1952, pp. 356-373. It is important to remember that very many of the people in these four lists were not themselves Quakers.

SCHOOLS AND OTHER INSTITUTIONS

78 Varieties of schools Friends' schools may be roughly classified into three groups: (a) meeting schools; (b) private schools; and (c) 'public' schools (which, in view of different, but equally misleading, terminology in England and America, will be referred to as committee schools). The fact that a boy or girl was at a Friends' school of any category is no proof of membership.

79 Meeting schools From the 17th century a number of meetings invited a schoolmaster to teach school on the meeting house premises, leaving him after appointment to make his own financial arrangements. Few of these survived into the 19th century and the most noteworthy to continue into the 20th were Friends School, Lancaster and Stramongate School, Kendal.

80 Private schools There is no comprehensive list of the very extensive number of private schools run by individual Friends in the 18th and 19th centuries. In very few cases are there lists of pupils, though a few (for example Grove House, Tottenham; Joseph Tatham's, Leeds and Isaac Payne's, Epping) have survived. Originals or photocopies have been acquired by Friends House Library and indexes are available.

81 Committee schools In 1702 London Friends set up the Clerkenwell school and workhouse (which became in 1786 Islington Road School), in 1825 Croydon, and in 1879 Saffron Walden. Other committee schools were: Ackworth (1779); Sidcot (1808); Wigton (1815, closed 1984); Lawrence Street, after 1846 Bootham, York (1823, taken over by Yorkshire quarterly meeting 1829); Castlegate, after 1857 the Mount, York (1831); Rawdon (1832, closed 1921); Penketh (1834, closed 1934); Ayton (1841, closed 1997); Sibford (1842); and, in a different category,

Leighton Park, Reading (1890). In Ireland there were three 'province schools': Lisburn (1774); Mountmellick (1786, closed 1921); and Newtown (1798); together with Brookfield Agricultural School (1836, closed 1921).

For most, if not all, of these schools admissions books were maintained and in many cases subsequently printed, though not always with the full particulars of the manuscript. In other cases (for example Bootham, Sidcot) printed registers were issued, containing biographical information supplied by old scholars in response to questionnaires. Alphabetical indexes, compiled from the admissions books, are available at Friends House Library for Ackworth 1779-1979, Ayton 1841-1998, Penketh 1834-1934, Rawdon 1832-82, Sibford 1842-67, and Wigton 1815-1953. Numbers range from 1,120 (Rawdon) to over 18,000 (Ackworth). A handlist on sources giving information on Quaker schools in Britain and Ireland is available from Friends House Library.

82 Other educational institutions The Flounders Institute, Ackworth, was opened in 1848 for the training of Friend teachers, generally those serving as apprentices in one of the committee schools. In 1894 it moved to Leeds to be near the Yorkshire College. In 1909 it was discontinued, income being allocated to the provision of exhibitions and grants. A record of individuals will be found in the *List of trustees, governors, principals, tutors and students 1848-1930*, 1931: it will be recognised that this includes some Friends who received exhibitions after the institution closed.

In 1876 a group of Manchester Friends founded Dalton Hall for Quaker students, and later for others, associated with Friends, also attending Owens College, later the University of Manchester. It ceased as an official responsibility of Friends in 1957. In 1903 Woodbrooke, Selly Oak, Birmingham, was opened as a centre for adult education and religious, social and international study. It was the first of a group of Selly Oak colleges, including Kingsmead (1905), Westhill (1907) and Fircroft (1909). A typescript list of members of Woodbrooke staff is available at Friends House Library.

83 The Retreat, York In 1796 a group of Quakers opened The Retreat, York, a 'retired habitation' for Friends 'who may be in a state of Lunacy or so deranged in mind as to require such a provision'. An extensive archive, deposited at the Borthwick Institute of Historical Research, York, includes minute books, visitors books, admission and medical records, and general correspondence. Patient records less than 100 years old are closed. Bloomfield Hospital, a similar institution established in Dublin by Irish Friends, was opened in 1812.

MISCELLANEOUS SOURCES OF INFORMATION

84 *Piety promoted*; *Annual monitor* In 1701 there was printed the first part of *Piety promoted* which aimed at being 'a collection of dying sayings' but also contained useful biographical notices. The eleventh part was published in 1829. A four volume 1854 Philadelphia edition is (though not the best textually) probably the most convenient for general use: it carries notices for some 680 Friends and an alphabetical index is available in Friends House Library. From 1813 to 1919/20 the *Annual monitor* carried a substantial list of deaths of Friends in the British Isles. Joseph J. Green in *Quaker records*, 1894, provides an index to over 20,000 names (with ages and place of death) in the *Annual monitor* 1813-1892. This is supplemented by two typescript indexes at Friends House Library covering 1893-1901 and 1902-1919/20. These indexes are useful not only for specific names but for indicating where a particular family lived. The *Annual monitor* also carried shorter or longer obituaries of some 3,100 Friends: an index of these is available in Friends House Library.

85 *The Friend*; *The British Friend* Two Quaker periodicals were started in 1843, *The Friend* then taking an 'evangelical' line and *The British Friend* then taking a 'conservative' one. *The Friend* included notices of marriages and deaths from the outset and of births from 1850; *The British Friend* (which ceased in 1913) included notices of births, marriages and deaths from 1845; report of non-usage marriages should not be expected in either journal before 1859. From 1894 *The Friend* started to carry obituary notices on a regular basis: an index to some 3,600 obituaries 1894-1980 is available in Friends House Library.

86 Non-Quaker sources It is not necessary here to refer in detail to sources which would be followed up for any person, Friend or non-Friend. Wills, as already mentioned (§55), were proved in the appropriate ecclesiastical court, or from 1858 in the civil courts, in the usual way. If the executors were (as they normally would be) Quakers, they would be unable before the Affirmation Act 1696 (7 & 8 Will. 3 c. 34) to swear an affidavit; and as many Friends were uneasy at the wording of the affirmation in that act, some Friends were unable to affirm in the required form until the Affirmation Act 1722 (8 Geo. 1 c. 6). In some instances the clerk of the court made specific note that an affirmation had been made; in others (though it must be presumed that an oath was not taken) he wrote 'jurat' as with other wills. The entry 'jurat' must not therefore be taken as evidence that the executors were not Quakers.

Non-Quaker sources which should be consulted in relation to entries in the books of sufferings (§§ 63-4) include such civil records as quarter sessions books and such ecclesiastical records as presentments.

87 Dictionary of Quaker biography In 1959 Friends House Library began the compilation, largely through voluntary help, of a typescript dictionary of Quaker biography (DQB). William Bacon Evans (1875-1964) of Philadelphia had spent a number of years preparing biographical notes on Friends and after his death these were typed by the Quaker Collection, Haverford College Library (WBE). The typescript DQB-WBE is available, in a single alphabet, both at Haverford College and in Friends House Library. There are now about 25,000 entries. It is not regarded as more than a working document.

88 Leeds database Russell and Jean Mortimer constructed a card index of biographical data on several thousand Friends in Leeds and the surrounding area and in the 1980s Arthur Olver indexed a substantial number of minute books and other records of Brighouse, Knaresborough and Settle monthly meetings. The records indexed are all deposited in the Brotherton Library, University of Leeds, which has received a grant to create databases for these resources, enabling retrieval by name, place, date and meeting, thus making an unrivalled source for historical and biographical work on West Riding Friends.

89 Family histories A substantial number of histories of families, either Quaker or formerly Quaker, are likely to have information confirming or supplementing that available from the registers. Friends in general did not make use of coats of arms, those early Quakers who might be entitled to them quietly dropping them.

90 Portraits Until the mid-19th century Quakers officially shunned portraits, fearing that they might untruthfully flatter and 'exalt the creature'. Though more Friends than might have been supposed did in fact sit for painters, many if not most reputed portraits of early Quakers are spurious: see John L. Nickalls, *Some Quaker portraits, certain and uncertain* (Friends Historical Society supplement 29), 1958. From the mid-18th century silhouettes, however, were felt to be safe. Ever fascinated by new technology, Friends in the mid-19th century welcomed photography and, innocently unaware of future developments, believed it unerringly truthful. They therefore had no scruples in being photographed and the development of the *carte de visite*, at reasonable cost, encouraged them.

APPENDIX A:

DIGEST REGISTERS - EXPLANATION OF CONTENTS; LISTS OF THE 1840-2 QUARTERLY MEETINGS

The notes in the first part of this appendix attempt no more than to draw the attention of users of the digests to some of the experience gained over the years by other users.

BIRTHS DIGEST

Columns 1, 2: 'Book, Page' : The reference is to the original registers as listed in the 1841 report of the Registrar General's office. The registers, now at the Public Record Office, have a revised numerical series. If entries are in identical form in more than one register there will be two (or more) bracketed figures in the digest. If entries are in more than one register but are different in spelling or in information given, there will be two (or more) entries in the digest.

Column 3: 'Name': No comment seems required.

Column 4: 'Date of birth': Appendix B should be consulted for all pre-1752 entries. The entry runs 'Year, Month, Day': in a few instances month and day may have been transposed in error.

Column 5: 'Place of birth': This should be compared with column 7 ('Parents abode') since the birth may be at some other place (for example the home of the wife's mother).

Column 6: 'Names of parents': If the father is deceased the entry does not always make this clear.

Column 7: 'Parents abode': If there is no entry under column 4 ('Place of birth') care should be taken not to state that the birth was at the place stated as the parents' abode: it may usually be true, but it is not necessarily so.

Column 8: 'Occupation': No special comment appears necessary, save that it is valuable to note any change of stated occupation at the births of different children.

Column 9: 'Monthly meeting': It is important to be clear that this refers to the monthly meeting responsible for surrendering the register. It may be the style of the monthly meeting at the time of birth, particularly in 19th century entries; but because of changes in style following amalgamations of monthly meetings, the likelihood is that it was not the name of the monthly meeting at the time that the birth entry was made.

Column 10: 'NM for non-member': (see §47) . Children, both of whose parents were in membership at the time of birth, had until 1959 a right to membership. The entry 'NM' indicates that a child, while not having that right, had some claim to be under the care of Friends. In general this tended to be where one parent only was in membership: in some cases, however, 'NM' was entered where neither parent appears to have been in membership - perhaps because one parent had been disowned for marriage before the priest to a non-Friend.

MARRIAGES DIGEST

Columns 1, 2: 'Book', 'Page': The notes for BIRTHS DIGEST columns 1, 2 apply.

Column 3: 'Name': No comment seems required.

Column 4: 'Residence': No comment seems required.

Column 5: 'Description': In London entries beginning 'Citizen and ...' care should be taken as the following word probably indicates the livery company to which the man belonged, rather than necessarily his actual occupation.

Column 6: 'Names of parents': In some cases the name of a stepmother is given (for example 'John and Hannah', rather than 'John and Mary (deceased)').

Column 7: 'Parents abode' : No comment seems required.

Column 8: 'To whom married - Name, Residence': It should be borne in mind that the digests of marriages give entries under each party and that fuller particulars are likely to be found by looking up the other entry.

Column 9: 'Where married': No comment seems required.

Column 10: 'Date of marriage': The notes for BIRTHS DIGEST column 4 apply.

Column 11: 'Monthly meeting': The notes for BIRTHS DIGEST column 9 apply.

BURIALS DIGEST

Columns 1, 2: 'Book', 'Page' : The notes for BIRTHS DIGEST columns 1, 2 apply.

Column 3: 'Name': No comment seems required.

Column 4: 'Date of death': The notes for BIRTHS DIGEST column 4 apply. Where no date is given column 9 ('Date of burial') should be consulted.

Column 5: 'Age': This is, with Quaker caution, prefixed by 'about': this may indicate a conviction that on only one day in the year can the precise age be true; it may also indicate an uncertainty of age of (say) two years either way.

Column 6: 'Residence': Care should be taken not to assume that this is the place of death. Where, after the 1840s, The Friend and British Friend give the place of death it is frequently found to have been when away from home. Though mobility may have been less in earlier times, evidence indicates that a number of Friends died while on family visits or attending the yearly meeting.

Column 7: 'Description': The phrase 'out of business' should normally be construed as 'retired': Quakers had, in general, a dislike to the term 'gentleman' for one of independent means.

Column 8: 'Monthly meeting': The notes for BIRTHS DIGEST column 9 apply.

Column 9: 'Date of burial': No comment seems required.

Column 10: 'Place of burial': If this differs by any considerable distance from the entry in column 6 ('Residence') it may indicate that further research is needed: it is always worth comparing these two columns.

Column 11: 'NM for non-member': The question of the interment of non-members in Friends burial grounds arose particularly in relation to disowned persons, more especially when their spouses were still in membership.

Regulations adopted by yearly meeting 1774 provided that 'when any person, not a member of the society, is permitted to be buried in friends burying-ground, it is to be noted in the margin of the register'. The book of discipline adopted in 1833 made more explicit provision for 'one or more proper persons' to be appointed by the monthly meeting, without whose authority 'no burial is to take place': as far as the burial of non-members was concerned, discipline stated that 'Friends are to exercise discretion in complying with any application'.

QUARTERLY MEETINGS AS EXISTING IN 1840-2

The name of the quarterly meeting is followed in brackets by the terminal dates of the digests for that quarterly meeting overall, including the supplements. This includes some retrospective anomalies with dates as early as 1575 and as late as 1841 (see §11). Events dated before about 1650 or after 1837 will be few and exceptional. This list indicates when the duplicate set of digest registers is known to be available in a record office or other public repository, with the call numbers following in brackets. Notes are also given where a digest register is known to contain entries relating to another pre-1974 county than that indicated in the title of the quarterly meeting, or where it lacks such entries as might be expected.

Beds & Herts QM (1645-1838): Available at Hertfordshire Archives and Local Studies (NQ1/5B/1 and 2, 5C/1, 5D/1). Entries for the Bishop's Stortford area may be found in the Essex QM digests; those for the south (for example Flamstead End) in London & Middlesex QM; those for the south-west (for example Watford, Rickmansworth) in Buckinghamshire QM.

Berks & Oxon QM (1612-1837): Available at Berkshire Record Office (D/F2 A/20, 21, 22).

Bristol & Somerset QM (1644-1837): Available at Bristol Record Office (SF/R1/1-6). A number of Bristol Friends lived within the compass of Frenchay monthly meeting and entries may be found in the Gloucester & Wilts QM digests.

Buckinghamshire QM (1645-1837): Available at Bedfordshire and Luton Archives and Record Service (FR2/10/5/44-46). The digests include entries for south-west Hertfordshire (for example Watford, Rickmansworth). Some entries for the Tring area may be found in the Beds & Herts QM digest.

Cambs & Hunts QM (1631-1841): Available at Cambridgeshire County Record Office, Cambridge (R82/15, R95/36). The area in north-east Huntingdonshire, in the neighbourhood of King's Cliffe, was at different times in the area of this quarterly meeting; of Lincolnshire QM; of Northamptonshire QM; and of Warwick, Leicester & Rutland QM.

Cheshire & Staffs QM (1648-1837): Available at Cheshire Record Office (EFC 1/14/1, 2, 3, 4). There is a deficiency of entries for south-east Staffordshire (in the neighbourhood of Wolverhampton). North-west Derbyshire (for example Low Leighton) is included.

Cornwall QM (1609-1837): Available at Cornwall Record Office (D.D.SF. 223 i, ii, iii, 224). Reference should be made to Hugh Peskett, *Guide to the parish and non-parochial registers of Devon and Cornwall 1538-1837* (Devon and Cornwall Record Society extra series 2), 1979, pp. 213-217. 222-224, 226-228.

Cumberland & Northumberland QM (1648-1837): Entries for south-east Cumberland (for example Penrith) will be found in the Westmorland digests QM; those for eastern Northumberland (for example Newcastle upon Tyne) in Durham QM.

Derby & Notts QM (1632-1837): Available at Nottinghamshire Archives (Q463-465). Entries for north-west Derbyshire (for example Low Leighton) will be found in the Cheshire & Staffs QM digests; those for northern Leicestershire (for example Castle Donington), while mainly in these digests, may also be found in Warwick, Leicester & Rutland QM; those for northern Derbyshire (for example Eckington, near Sheffield) may be found in Yorkshire QM.

Devonshire QM (1627-1837): Reference should be made to Hugh Peskett, *Guide to the parish and non parochial registers of Devon and Cornwall 1538-1837* (Devon and Cornwall Record Society extra series 2), 1979, pp. 217-221, 224-228.

Dorset & Hants QM (1638-1837): Available at Hampshire Record Office (24 M 54/25, 26).

Durham QM (1588-1841): Entries for northern Yorkshire (Richmond monthly meeting) may be found in these digests, or in those for Yorkshire QM, or those for Westmorland QM. Entries for north-east Yorkshire (Guisborough monthly meeting) may be found in these digests or in those for Yorkshire QM. These digests contain entries relating to eastern Northumberland (for example Newcastle upon Tyne).

Essex QM (1613-1837): Available at Essex University Library, Wivenhoe, Colchester. Entries for the Bishop's Stortford area of Hertfordshire are included in these digests; those for south-west Essex (for example Waltham Abbey, Barking) will be found in London & Middlesex QM.

Gloucester & Wilts QM (1642-1837): Available at Gloucestershire Record Office (D 1340 : A1/R1-4). Entries for north-east Gloucestershire (for example Stow-on-the-Wold, Chipping Campden) will be found in Warwick, Leicester & Rutland QM).

Hereford, Worcester & Wales GM (1635-1838): Available at Worcestershire Record Office, Worcester (898.2 : 1303/23-25). Entries for north-east and south-east Worcestershire (for example Stourbridge, Dudley; Shipston-on-Stour) are more likely to be found in Warwick, Leicester & Rutland QM).

Kent QM (1646-1837): A number of Friends living in north-west Kent had their membership in meetings belonging to London & Middlesex QM or, in a few cases, Sussex & Surrey QM.

Lancashire QM (1635-1838): Swarthmore monthly meeting was transferred from Lancashire to Westmorland about 1805: entries may be found in either digests. Parts of western Yorkshire and eastern Lancashire (for example Mankinholes, Todmorden) were transferred from Brighouse monthly meeting to Marsden monthly meeting about 1795: entries may be found either in the Lancashire QM or the Yorkshire QM digests.

Lincolnshire QM (1632-1837): Available at Lincolnshire Archives (Society of Friends 152-155). Refer to Cambs & Hunts QM for note on entries relating to south-west Lincolnshire (e g: Stamford) in relation to King's Cliffe.

London & Middlesex QM (1644-1838): Southwark (until 1800 Horsleydown) monthly meeting including parts of north-west Kent was always a part of London and Middlesex. The monthly meeting which included Kingston, Wandsworth and Croydon was transferred to London & Middlesex QM from Surrey QM in 1802; entries may be found either in London & Middlesex QM or in Sussex & Surrey QM.

Norfolk & Norwich QM (1613-1837): Available at Norfolk Record Office (SF 42, 43, 44, 45). North-east Suffolk (Beccles/Pakefield) is included in Norfolk; entries for the Brandon-Thetford area may be found in either Norfolk QM or Suffolk QM.

Northamptonshire QM (1647-1837): Available at Northamptonshire Record Office. No particular comment: refer to Cambs & Hunts QM for note on entries relating to north-east Northamptonshire (for example Duddington) in relation to King's Cliffe.

Suffolk QM (1641-1837): Available at Suffolk Record Office, Ipswich (FK 6/4/1-4). Entries relating to northern Suffolk (for example Beccles/Pakefield) will be found in Norfolk & Norwich QM; those for the Brandon-Thetford area may be found in either Suffolk QM or Norfolk QM.

Sussex & Surrey QM (1640-1837): The monthly meeting including Kingston, Wandsworth and Croydon was transferred from Surrey QM to London &

Middlesex QM in 1802 and entries may be found in Sussex & Surrey QM or in London & Middlesex QM digests.

Warwick, Leicester & Rutland QM (1623-1837) Entries for north-east and south-east Worcestershire (Stourbridge, Dudley; Shipston-on-Stour) are more likely to be found in these digests than in those for Hereford, Worcester & Wales GM. Entries for north-east Gloucestershire (for example Stow on-the-Wold, Chipping Campden) are included in these digests. Refer to Cambs & Hunts QM for note on entries made by Oakham monthly meeting (Rutland) in relation to King's Cliffe: in 1713 Oakham monthly meeting assumed part-responsibility for the meetings at Bourne and Stamford, Lincs.

Westmorland QM (1617-1837): Sedbergh monthly meeting (north-west Yorkshire) was always a constituent meeting of Westmorland QM. Entries for the Furness district of Lancashire (Swarthmore monthly meeting) may he found in either the Westmorland QM or Lancashire QM digests. The Westmorland QM digests contain entries for south-west Cumberland (for example Penrith). Entries relating to north Yorkshire (Richmond monthly meeting) may be found in Westmorland QM, Yorkshire QM or Durham QM.

Yorkshire QM (1575-1840): Entries for north Yorkshire (Richmond monthly meeting) may be found in these digests or in those for Westmorland QM or Durham QM. Entries for north-east Yorkshire (Guisborough monthly meeting) may be found in these digests or in those for Durham QM. Parts of western Yorkshire and eastern Lancashire (for example Mankinholes, Todmorden) were transferred from Brighouse monthly meeting to Marsden monthly meeting about 1795: entries may be found in the Yorkshire QM or the Lancashire QM digests.

The full set of Digest Registers for England and Wales to 1837 preserved at
Friends House have been microfilmed and published. A complete set is available
at the Society of Genealogists, London; films may also be available in libraries and
record offices in addition to those named here.

APPENDIX B :

DATES IN PRE-1752 QUAKER DOCUMENTS

1.Until 1751 the English (and Welsh) year began on Lady Day (25 March).

2.For Quakers, who eschewed the pagan names of the days and months, March was therefore first month and February twelfth month. Care is sometimes needed in, for example, post-1752 printing of earlier Quaker journals and the like where 'old style' dating has been silently translated into 'new style'. In the Digest Registers, however, the 1840-2 copyists continued the old style dating of the original.

3.It is often helpful, in copying from the registers, to make assurance doubly sure by using the old style numbers and the new style names in square brackets:

> 9 ii [April] 1731   12 x [December] 1740

It should be borne in mind that up to 1751 Quakers had no objection to September, October, November and December which were factual statements of the 7th, 8th, 9th and 10th months old style. From 1752 they *did* object to using these names which, though not associated with pagan deities, were in new style untruthful.

1.January and February present slightly greater complications and it is useful to indicate the year both in old style and new style, even where it is not double-dated in the original:

2.   7th 11 mo 1742 may be shown 7 xi 1742 [Jan 1742/3]

3.The first 24 days of March present even greater complications. Very often these are double-dated:

4.   15th 1st mo 1708/9

5.Where they are single-dated it is usually, but by no means always, in anticipation of the year which is to begin on 25 March:

> 7th 1mo 1737 is probably 7 i [March] 1736/7

Apart from variations in principle as regards the first 24 days of March, it is, of course, important to make allowances for ordinary human failure to remember to write the correct date early on in a new year.

1.It should be noticed that John Nickalls (*The journal of George Fox*, 1952, 1975, pp. xiii-xiv) judges that the first 24 days of March were normally reckoned part of the old year, whereas D.J. Steel, (*Sources for nonconformist genealogy and family history*, 1973, pp. 638-9) judges that they were normally reckoned part of the new. 'The Quaker calendar' by Samuel G. Barton (*Proc. Amer. Philosph. Soc.* vol. 93, 1949, pp. 32-9) argues that the Quaker year began on 1 March rather than 25 March, and a note in an Ifield and Shipley register (printed in *Sussex Arch. Coll.* vol. 55, 1912, p 81) lends substance to this:

2.'....the year is.... to Begin the First day of the First Month commonly called march Whereas in the worlds Accompt it begins not till the 25th day of the said Month.'

3.From 1752 the English year began on 1 January. So, in theory, for Quakers 10th month 1751 should be followed by 1st month 1752: it is scarcely necessary to add, resistance to change being what it is, that a fair number of entries for 11th and 12th month 1751 are to be found.

4.It was provided by 'Chesterfield's Act' (24 Geo. 2 c. 23) that 2 September 1752 should be followed by 14 September. It must not, however, be assumed that 'new style' was everywhere adopted, or immediately adopted: in the 20th century a Norfolk woman was known to say that she 'was born on old May day'. In consulting modern printed sources care should be exercised as some writers correct the year for January, February and March 1-24 without further alteration, while others bring the whole date into new style by adding 10 days for 17th century dates and 11 days for those of the 18th century.

5.

APPENDIX C :

LONDON YEARLY MEETING QUERIES 1742

1.What present prisoners?

2.How many discharged since last year, when and how?

3.How many died prisoners?

4.How many meeting houses built, and what meetings new settled?

5.How many publick friends died and when?

6.What is the state of your meeting? Is there any Growth in the Truth? And doth any Convincement appear since last year? And is Love and Unity preserved amongst you?

7.Is it your Care, by Example and Precept, to Train up children in all Godly Conversation, and in the frequent reading of the Holy Scripture as also in Plainness of Speech, Behaviour and Apparel?

8.Do you bear a faithful and Christian testimony against the Receiving or Paying tithes? and against Bearing of Arms? and do you admonish such as are unfaithful therein?

9.Do you stand clear in our Testimony against Defrauding the King of his Customs, Duties or Excise, or in Dealing in Goods Suspected to be Run?

10.How are the Poor among you provided for? and what care is taken of the education of their offspring?

11.Do you keep a record in your Quarterly and Monthly Meetings, of the Prosecutions and Sufferings of your Respective members? and have you a Record for your Meeting houses, Burial grounds, etc?

12.For a full account, with all variants in the text, of the queries, see 'Friends' queries and general advices: a survey of their development in London yearly meeting 1682-1928' by Richard E. Stagg in *J. Friends Hist. Soc.* vol. 49 (1959-61) pp. 209-235, 249-269, 279

APPENDIX D:

TRANSCRIPTS OF MINUTE BOOKS

1.*The minute book of the monthly meeting of the Society of Friends for the Upperside of Buckinghamshire, 1669-1690.* Transcribed ... by Beatrice Saxon Snell. (Buckinghamshire Archaeological Society, Records Branch, 1). 1937.

2.*The first minute book of the Gainsborough Monthly Meeting of the Society of Friends, 1669-1719.* Edited by Harold W. Brace. (Lincoln Record Society, 38, 40, 44). 3 vols., 1948-1951.

3.*Minute book of the Men's Meeting of the Society of Friends in Bristol, 1667-1686; 1686-1704.* Edited by Russell Mortimer. (Bristol Record Society, 26, 30). 2 vols., 1971, 1977.

4.*Society of Friends: Kingston Men's Monthly Meeting book, 1667-1691.* Transcribed by Joan Wilkins. Reproduced from typescript, 1975.

5.*The Somersetshire Quarterly Meeting of the Society of Friends, 1668-1699.* Edited by Stephen C. Morland. (Somerset Record Society, 75). 1978.

6.*Leeds Friends' minute book, 1692 to 1712.* Edited by Jean and Russell Mortimer. (Yorkshire Archaeological Society, Record Series, 139). 1980.

The following typed transcripts are available in Friends House Library:

7.Berkshire minutes, transcribed by Beatrice and Nina Saxon Snell, as follows:- QM minutes 1669-1730 (1679-1681 not extant); Reading MM 1668-1716 (includes Curtis party minutes from 1683 until the cessation of the separation in 1716); Reading MM 1685-1730 (orthodox); Windsor MM 1668-1755; Newbury and Oare MM 1674-1723; Vale of White Horse MM 1673-1722; Vale of White Horse

Women's MM 1676-1730. This completes the main series of Berkshire minutes to the 1720s.

8.Derbyshire minutes, transcribed by Joan Goodwin, as follows: - Chesterfield MM 1691-1732.

9.Lincolnshire minutes, transcribed by Norman Leveritt: Spalding MM 1714-1742/3.

10.London and Middlesex minutes, transcribed by Beatrice and Nina Saxon Snell, as follows:- Longford MM 1670-1730. London and Middlesex minutes transcribed by Craig W. Horle as follows:- Six weeks meeting minutes 1671 -1692/3; Meeting of twelve minutes 1679-1682.

11.Oxfordshire minutes, transcribed by Beatrice and Nina Saxon Snell, as follows:- QM minutes 1671-1730; Witney MM 1675-1704; Warborough MM 1670-1771 (1716-1737 not extant). Minutes of Banbury MM are not extant to 1736.

12.Somersetshire minutes, transcribed by Stephen C. Morland, as follows:- Ilchester (from 1691 South Somerset) MM 1668-1699; Mid Somerset MM 1691-1699 (formed out of Ilchester MM 1691); West Somerset MM 1676-1699; North Somerset MM 1667-1699. This, with 5, completes the main series of Somerset records to 1699.

13.Wiltshire minutes, transcribed by Beatrice and Nina Saxon Snell, as follows:- QM minutes 1678-1730; Chippenham MM 1669-1725; Charlcote MM 1677-1705, 1709-1730 (1706-1708 wanting); Lavington (Southern) MM 1704-1738. This completes the main series of Wiltshire minutes to the 1720s.

APPENDIX E:

EDITIONS OF THE BOOK OF DISCIPLINE TO 1900

Britain

1738 'Christian and brotherly advices, given forth from time to time by the yearly meetings in London, alphabetically digested under proper heads'. Copied in manuscript for clerks of quarterly and monthly meetings; additions were made over the ensuing 40 years, but it must not be supposed that the same additions were made to each copy.

1782 *Extracts from the minutes and advices of the yearly meeting of Friends held in London, from its first institution,* 1783.

An *Appendix* was printed in 1792

1801 *Extracts from the minutes and advices of the yearly meeting of Friends held in London, from its first institution,* 1802

A supplement was printed in 1822

1833 *Rules of discipline of the religious Society of Friends, with advices, being extracts from the minutes and epistles of their yearly meeting held in London from its first institution,* 1834.

1861 *Extracts from the minutes and epistles of the yearly meeting of the religious Society of Friends held in London from its first institution to the present time, relating to Christian doctrine, practice and discipline,* 1861. This was the first revision to depart from alphabetical into chapter order

1883 *Book of Christian discipline of the Religious Society of Friends in Great Britain, consisting of extracts on doctrine, practice and church government,* 1883. This was the last revision before 1900

Ireland

1811   *Advices and rules agreed to by the yearly meeting of Friends in Ireland,* 1811. A supplement was published in 1830.

1841   *Rules of discipline of the yearly meeting of Friends in Ireland, with advices issued and adopted thereby,* 1841.

1864   *Advices and minutes issued and adopted by the yearly meeting of Friends in Ireland in relation to Christian doctrine, practice and discipline,* 1864.

APPENDIX F :

ADOPTIONS

There is no adoption society in connection with the Society of Friends. Children adopted by Quaker parents will have no entry in the digest of births (unless the child itself was of Quaker parents). It is unusual for adoptions to be recorded in the 'Births, marriages and deaths' columns of *The Friend* (§85) until the later 1930s.

Belief by people that they were adopted 'under the auspices of the Quakers' persists, together with a recollection of having been at Friends House in childhood and introduced to the adoptive parents. The probable reason for such belief is that, from 1940 until 1962, a juvenile court was held each Tuesday on Friends House premises, and adoption orders would have been made at the court. It was known from 1940 until 1956 as 'Friends House Juvenile Court' and thereafter as 'North London Juvenile Court'. Its records have now (1999) passed from the Camden Juvenile Court to the London Metropolitan Archives, 40 Northampton Road, London EC1R 0HB, to whom enquirers must write in advance.

INDEX

Note that the references are to section numbers not pages